Jazz

Michael Burnett

Oxford University Press
Music Department,
Walton Street, Oxford OX2 6DP

Contents

1 The roots of jazz
Jazz old and new 4
Where jazz started 5
The music of the slaves 5
Instruments used by the slaves 5
Questions 6
Where jazz came from 7
Spirituals 7
Worksongs 8
The Blues 9
Questions and projects 9, 10

2 Jazz is born
New Orleans 12
'The hottest music in the world' 12
How jazz began 13
Ragtime 13
Jelly Roll Morton 14
'A city full of the sounds of music' 14
Projects and questions 14, 15
Jazz travels north 16
'We couldn't play soft' 16
The New Orleans Rhythm Kings 17
Boogie-woogie 18
'I'm so hungry . . . I can't hardly speak' 18
Questions and projects 19

3 Swing, be-bop and modern jazz
Jitterbugs and bobbysoxers 21
Swing arrangements 21
Benny Goodman 22
Questions and project 23
Be-bop 24
'Dig them new sounds, man' 25
Playing it cool 26
Questions and projects 26
Modern jazz 27
Third stream 27

The new wave 28
Experimental sounds 28
Jazz today 29
The traditional jazz band 29
Swing bands 30
Small bands 30
Trios 31
Free-form jazz 31
Jazz-pop bands 31
Questions and projects 32

4 Jazz instruments
Woodwind 34
Brass 35
Strings 36
Percussion 37
Amplification 37
Jazz singers 38
Questions and projects 39

5 Jazz and other kinds of music
Jazz and popular music 41
Musicals 41
Irving Berlin 42
Writing songs for fun 42
Questions and project 43
Jazz and classical music 44
The threepenny opera 44
Bix Beiderbecke 44
George Gershwin 44
Porgy and Bess 45
Down on Catfish Row 46
Picnic on Kittiwah Island 46
West Side Story 47
Project and questions 48

Discography and resources Inside back cover

Slaves making music and dancing ▶

1 The roots of jazz

Jazz old and new

A famous jazz musician was once asked 'What is jazz?' He replied 'You see this trumpet. I play what I feel on it. That's jazz'. Jazz music has many different styles. It has been played for many years. But whatever the style, old or new, we can safely say that all jazz is based on feelings. When a jazz musician plays on stage he expresses his feelings, through his playing, to an audience. If he plays well then people in the audience share his feelings and respond to his message. One person, after hearing Duke Ellington's band, claimed 'I almost jumped out of the balcony. One piece excited me so much I screamed'. Someone else once described the trumpet-playing of Louis Armstrong like this:

> He started out building and building, finally reaching a full climax, ending on his high F . . . The rhythm was rocking . . . Everybody was standing up . . .

You'll read about Louis Armstrong in this book. You'll also read about how jazz began in New Orleans early this century, when it was called 'the hottest music in the world'. You'll learn about 'jitterbugs' and 'bobbysoxers', and about how jazz became 'cool'. But when reading about jazz in the past, we must remember that jazz is today's music as well. No-one reminds us of that better than the trumpeter **Miles Davis**. When he picks up his trumpet and 'plays what he feels', we realize that although jazz styles have changed the old excitement remains:

> It was as if Miles were leading his exploring party through a dense electronic rain forest. Sensing a clearing, Davis extends his fingers in a signal and his group halts motionless as the leader's trumpet slips ahead alone, reporting what he sees. Echoing, reverberating, electronically shaped notes and phrases form the strange beautiful foliage and strong life rhythms of Davis's musical world.

Miles Davis

Louis Armstrong

Where jazz started

During the 18th and 19th centuries thousands of people were taken as slaves from Africa to America. For these Africans life became a nightmare. Many died on the long voyage by sailing-ship. Those that survived were sold in auctions and put to work on the farms of the southern states of America. The nightmare of slavery was made worse when families which had travelled from Africa together were split up at these auctions. Children were taken from their parents and husbands from their wives, never to see each other again. Here are the words of a song which tells of just such a case:

> They sold my brother Sam to a man from Alabama,
> My sister went to Georgia far away.
> Then they broke my heart for life
> When they sold my loving wife
> In those agonising, cruel slavery days.

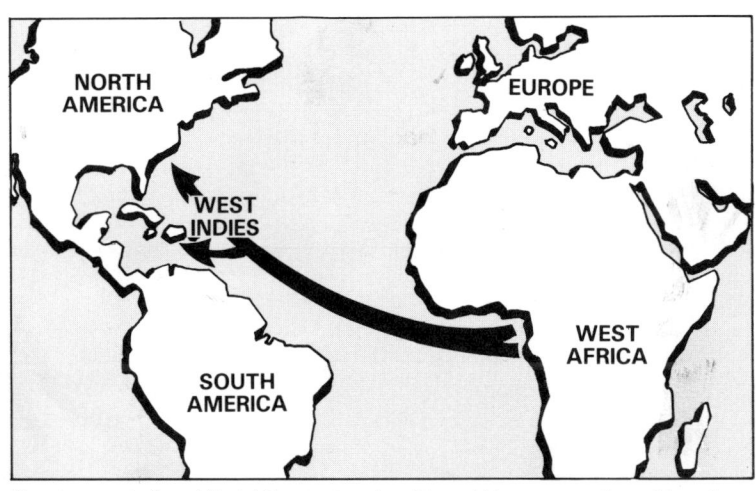

Slaves gathering cotton

The slave route from West Africa to America. Many Africans were also sold as slaves in the West Indies

Slavery was, indeed, a nightmare come true. And yet, in the middle of the nightmare, the African slaves played and sang music which later influenced music the world over. For in the music of the slaves we find the beginnings of jazz.

The music of the slaves

For the African, music is a way of life. It's not surprising, then, that making music played an important part in the lives of African slaves in America. In songs like the one above the slaves expressed unhappiness. They also had songs for healing the sick and lullabies for quietening babies. And whilst working in the fields, the slaves sang rhythmic tunes in time with their actions. (You can find such a worksong on page 10.)

Instruments used by the slaves

African music is famous for its exciting rhythms. These were often played on **drums,** since the drum is the most popular of African instruments. The slaves made drums of many different shapes and sizes. They played them in a variety of ways, for example with the palms of the hands, the finger tips, or with sticks.

Other percussion instruments modelled on those of Africa included **shakers** made from containers partly filled with pebbles, and **tambourines**. Sometimes the slaves wore anklets to which pieces of metal were fastened. As the slaves stamped or danced in time to the music, the jangling of the pieces of metal created off-beat rhythms. The bones of cattle were also turned into percussion instruments. Large beef-bones were banged together or used as drum-sticks. Jawbones became **scrapers** when the teeth were scraped with keys or other metal objects.

The slaves also made string instruments similar to those played in Africa. The most popular of these were the **fiddle** and **banjo**. The fiddle had the same structure as the violin. Often, though, it was carved rather differently, as we learn from this description of a slave instrument:

> On the top of the finger board was the figure of a man sitting down, with two pegs behind him to which the strings were fastened.

The fiddle was played with a curved bow made from wood and horse-hair. The banjo had four strings which were strummed with the fingers.

Questions

1. What was the purpose of taking thousands of people from Africa to America during the 18th and 19th centuries?
2. Why did music play an important part in the lives of the slaves?
3. Which is the most popular of African instruments?
4. How were jawbones turned into percussion instruments?
5. Which of these two instruments is played with a bow: fiddle, banjo?

African drummers

Where jazz came from

Slaves dancing—the large house in the background is where the plantation owner lives

As time went on, the music of the slaves was influenced by that of their European masters. The slaves sang European **hymn tunes**. They whistled popular European **march tunes**, which they heard being played by military **bands**. These bands took part in the American Civil War, which ended in 1865 with the freeing of all slaves. When some of the bands were split up after the war, many of their instruments found their way into the hands of newly-freed slaves. These instruments included **clarinets**, **cornets** and **trombones** (see pages 34-35). Soon most towns in the south of America had bands formed by groups of black people. And whether the occasion was a picnic or a dance, a riverboat trip or a funeral, it was accompanied by the sound of a brass band.

Spirituals

The firm beat of the march was echoed in the **spirituals** which black Americans sang at prayer meetings. These were religious songs, based on European hymn tunes. The singing was led by the preacher. As he sang, the congregation joined in with shouts of 'Yes, lawd' and 'Hallelujah'. They moved in time to

Singing spirituals

the music, too, clapping and stamping on the beat. Soon the shouts gave way to singing as the congregation took over the preacher's tune, or added harmonies to it. (You can still hear spirituals performed like this today by black congregations in the Southern states of America.)

Worksongs

Many spirituals referred to the railways which provided work for the freed slaves. But, whether they worked on the railroad track or in the fields, black Americans kept up the habit of singing as they worked. The rhythmic tunes they sang were led by one member of each group of workers. The leader sang a few words and then the rest of the group joined in with a chorus of 'Lawd, lawd, lawd' or 'Heave away'. Singing like this is described as **call and response** singing. Call and response singing is common in African music, but the tunes of **worksongs** were European in style.

Like spirituals, worksongs are still sung today. Here is a description of some 20th-century railroad workers:

> The hot Southern sun shines down on the brown and glossy muscles of the work gang. The picks make whirling rainbow arcs around the shoulders of the singers . . . The song leader now begins — pick handle twirling in his palms, the pickhead flashing in the sun:
> *Take this hammo — Huh!*
> The men grunt as the picks bite in together. They join the leader on his line, trailing in, one in harmony, one talking the words, another grunting them out between clenched teeth, another throwing out a high, thin cry above the rest . . .

A railroad work gang

The Blues

When the slaves were set free in 1865, they faced poverty and homelessness. The nightmare of slavery was over, but black people were often denied jobs and mistreated in other ways, as this old song tells us:

> I been hurt an' mistreated
> 'till I done made up my mind.
> I been hurt an' mistreated
> 'till I done made up my mind.
> Gonna leave dis ol' country
> An' all my troubles behind.

Those words come from a special kind of song called a **Blues**. 'Singing the Blues' has always been a way for black Americans to tell of the unhappy things in their lives. Whatever the notes of the tunes, all Blues songs are based on the same set of three chords (or groups of notes) in the backing. Originally these chords were played by the singer on a banjo or guitar. In the key of C, the three chords are C, F and G. Usually they are spaced out over 12 bars like this:

$\frac{4}{4}$ | C / / / | C / / / | C / / / | C / / / |

| F / / / | F / / / | C / / / | C / / / |

| G / / / | G / / / | C / / / | C / / / ||

The chords that make up the Blues are like a skeleton. Everyone has a skeleton inside their skin; but it's the flesh on top of the bones that makes the skeleton a person. In the same way, the Blues chords come alive because of what goes on top of them, the notes the singer adds. Each performer adds something different (although all Blues singers do what they call 'shove in cryin'' — that is, make a sad, mournful sound). This sad feeling is partly caused by the fact that singers slide certain notes deliberately in and out of tune. These notes are around the third and seventh steps of the scale, and are called **blue notes**.

Blind Lemon Jefferson was a famous early Blues singer. Later **Ma Rainey** and **Bessie Smith** became popular too. They were among the first to make Blues recordings in the 1920s.

Bessie Smith

Questions

1. What were the European influences on the music of the slaves?
2. Name the instruments used in military bands.
3. What is a spiritual?
4. What is 'call and response' singing?
5. How many different chords are there in the Blues?

Projects

1. Here is a worksong.
   Try singing it with one or two members of the group taking the part of the leader and the rest the work gang. Then play the tune through using any instruments you can find. Make the 'call and response' pattern clear by using different-sounding instruments for the leader and chorus parts. If there are any guitarists in your group they can play the chord shown above the tune. Some of you can play the accompaniment:

Leader *Em throughout*
Eight-een ham-mers stand-in' well in a line. Well

Chorus
Ah___ Well in a line.
⑤ eight-een ham-mers stand-in' well in a line.
Ah___ Well in a line.

play 4 times

count	① 2 3 4	② 2 3 4
instruments 1	b g	g b
instruments 2	E E	g E E

2. In the key of C the Blues chord sequence uses the chords of **C, F** and **G**. One version of the chord sequence is set out for you above. Higher-pitched instruments (such as melodicas) should play the Instruments 1 part. Lower-pitched instruments (such as bass xylophone or the bass part of the piano) should play Instruments 2:

count	① 2 3 4	② 2 3 4	③ 2 3 4	④ 2 3 4	⑤ 2 3 4	⑥ 2 3 4
instruments 1	C e g	C e g	C e g	C e g	F a c	F a c
instruments 2	C C	C C	C C	C C	C F	F F F

count	⑦ 2 3 4	⑧ 2 3 4	⑨ 2 3 4	⑩ 2 3 4	⑪ 2 3 4	⑫ 2 3 4
instruments 1	C e g	C e g	G b d	G b d	C e g	C e g
instruments 2	C C	C C	G G	G G	C C	C C

3. With the help of your teacher (or using your local library), get a copy of Volume II of the Folkways Jazz record series (see inside back cover for details of this). Listen to Ma Rainey's recording of *Hear me talkin' to you*, a Blues song which starts with a short, four bar introduction. As you listen count the number of times the Blues chord sequence is played before the song comes to an end. Also, see if you can hear the extra F chord which Ma Rainey's band play in bar 11 of the sequence (see Project 2). What happens during the fourth playing of the chord sequence? Do you think there are any home-made instruments in the band? Discuss these questions with members of your music group.

A street in New Orleans ▶

2 Jazz is born

New Orleans

New Orleans is a busy port in the American state of Louisiana. It is situated on the **Mississippi** river, about 100 miles from the sea. The city was built by French settlers and then taken over by Spain. France took back the city and eventually sold the whole state of Louisiana to the United States of America in 1803. By this time New Orleans was already rich through the export of cotton and sugar. Ships carried these goods to Europe. They then returned via West Africa, where they took slaves on board.

Famous river-boats, such as the 'Robert E. Lee', sailed north from New Orleans along the Mississippi to Memphis and St Louis. Called 'Ol' Man River', the Mississippi was the centre of New Orleans's commercial life. At the centre of the city's cultural life was its music.

A New Orleans marching band

'The hottest music in the world'

New Orleans was full of bars and dance-halls in which music was played. The city's annual carnival, **Mardi Gras**, was a feast of music and dancing which lasted for weeks. And brass bands could be heard everywhere:

> Such bands! Like yellow sunlight, the sweetly blatant, brassy sounds float through the streets, echo by day and by night from the old, balconied houses, resound in the dim courtyards, carrying the sound of the old marches . . .

These marches were played in a very exciting way by black musicians. In fact, their playing was so exciting that it was described as 'the hottest in the world'. Skipping, off-beat rhythms, like those found in spirituals (see page 7), were added to the march tunes. There were 'call and response' patterns (see page 8), with a solo instrument taking on the role of the leader and the rest of the instruments answering in chorus. And, throughout, the players used 'blue notes' (see page 9).

New Orleans, where jazz began

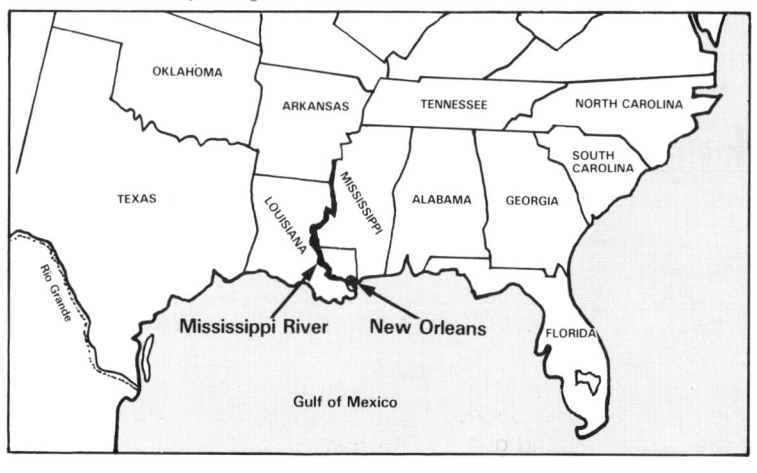

A riverboat band

How jazz began

The bands were led by the cornet, or trumpet player. His job was to play the tune. The clarinettist wove patterns of notes above and below the tune. And the trombonist made up his own part, based on the notes of the chords that went with it. The bass line was played on string bass, or tuba if it was a marching band. There were usually musicians playing piano (or banjo in marching bands), and drums, too. (For more about these instruments see pages 34-37.)

Sometimes two bands would turn up to play at the same dance-hall or street corner. Then there would be a sort of musical boxing-match. The bands would play different pieces at the same time. The one which knocked the other out, by making the loudest sound, was the winner. This meant that the band could stay and get paid for playing the concert. A popular job with musicians was playing in one of the bands on the Mississippi riverboats, too.

Of all the bands in New Orleans at the beginning of the century the one led by **Buddy Bolden** was the most popular. Buddy's cornet playing was astounding. He was even described as 'the blowingest thing since Gabriel'. (The angel Gabriel, in the Bible, was the angel who played the 'Last Trump', God's call to wake the dead.) As for Buddy's band, it 'killed all the other best bands in New Orleans'.

Soon the music played by the New Orleans bands became called **jazz**. No-one knows exactly when this word was first used, or where it came from. (One explanation is that jazz was named after a popular musician of the time called **Jazzbo Brown**.)

THE ENTERTAINER

Ragtime

Often, in the smaller bars in New Orleans, there wasn't room for a band. So music was provided by a pianist, who played **rags**. These were pieces with an 'oom-pah' left-hand part, on top of which the pianist played a lively tune full of off-beat rhythms. Usually the rags were written down and published. **Scott Joplin** became the most famous composer of them. (If you ever see the film *The Sting* you'll hear some of Joplin's rags, including *The Entertainer*, on the soundtrack.)

Hundreds of ragtime pieces by Scott Joplin and other composers were published between 1895 and 1910. Indeed, ragtime soon became a craze throughout America, and soon spread to Europe as well. Gramophone records had not been invented yet. But there were mechanical pianos instead. These were coin-operated, like today's juke-boxes. You put in your nickel and, magically, the piano played the latest ragtime hit.

Jelly Roll Morton

The most famous ragtime pianist in New Orleans was **Jelly Roll Morton**. Sometimes Jelly Roll used classical tunes in his rags. He was well known as a Blues player, too. Here's a description of him in action:

> Jelly Roll sat down . . . The floor shivered, the people swayed while he attacked the keyboard with his long, skinny fingers, beating out a double rhythm with his feet on the loud pedal . . .

Jelly Roll Morton

'A city full of the sounds of music'

Buddy Bolden and Jelly Roll Morton were the pop stars of their day. They excited people with their music just as much then as Elvis Presley or Blondie were to later in the century. For young people in particular, New Orleans must have been a really exciting place as jazz and ragtime developed. Guitarist Danny Barker grew up there at this time. Here he describes one of his most pleasant memories:

> A bunch of kids, playing, would suddenly hear sounds . . . but we wouldn't be sure where they were coming from . . . . So we'd start running . . . . The city was full of the sounds of music . . . .

Projects

1   Here is part of a piano rag tune by Scott Joplin:

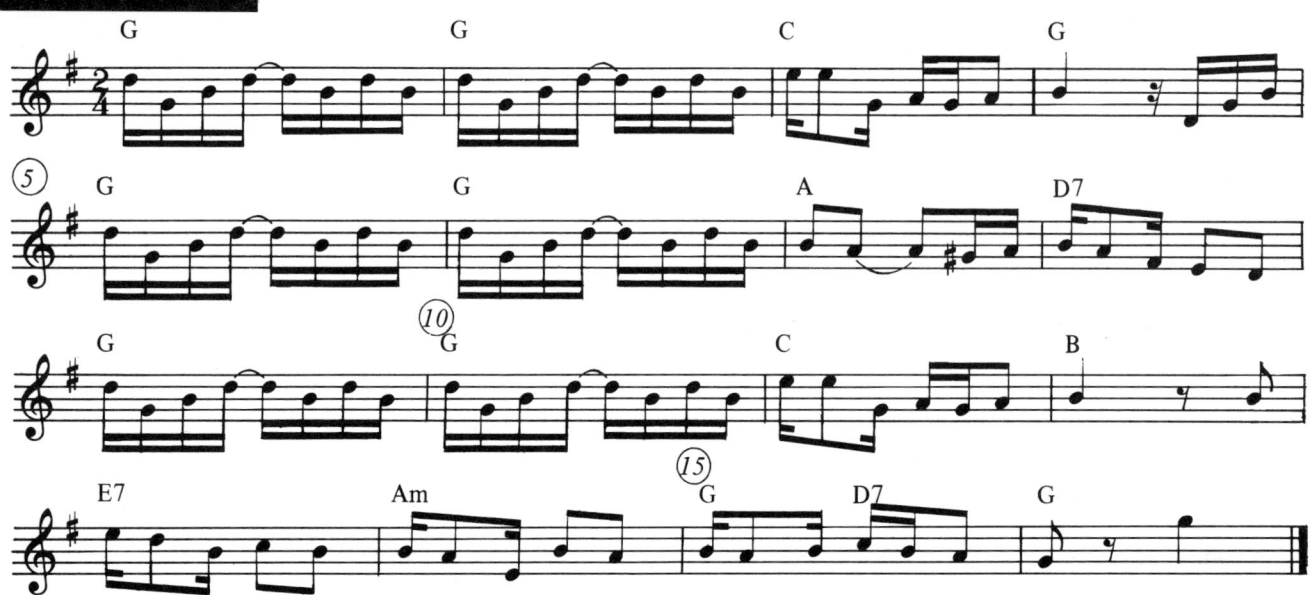

Play the tune through on melodicas, recorders or any other instruments you have available. Notice the catchy, off-beat rhythms typical of ragtime. Once you've practised the tune get a few members of the group to add this accompaniment to it, using the lowest-pitched instruments:

You'll find another Scott Joplin rag, *Maple Leaf Rag,* on the same album. The rag has been arranged for a band called the **New Orleans Feetwarmers.** Write out a list of instruments you hear being played on the recording.

If there are any guitarists in the group then they can provide another accompaniment for the tune by playing the chords which are shown above it.

2   With the help of your teacher (or using your local library), get a copy of Volume 11 of the Folkways Jazz record series (see inside back cover for details). Listen to Scott Joplin's *Original Rags,* a recording of a mechanical piano version made by the composer himself. You'll notice that the first of the rags begins with the tune set out in Project 1. Do you prefer your version or Scott Joplin's? Listen out for the 'oom-pah' left-hand part and lively right-hand rhythms of the piano version.

Questions

1   On which river is New Orleans situated?
2   What is New Orleans' annual carnival called?
3   Who was 'the blowingest man . . . since Gabriel'?
4   What was Scott Joplin famous for?
5   Who was New Orleans' most famous ragtime pianist?

Jazz travels north

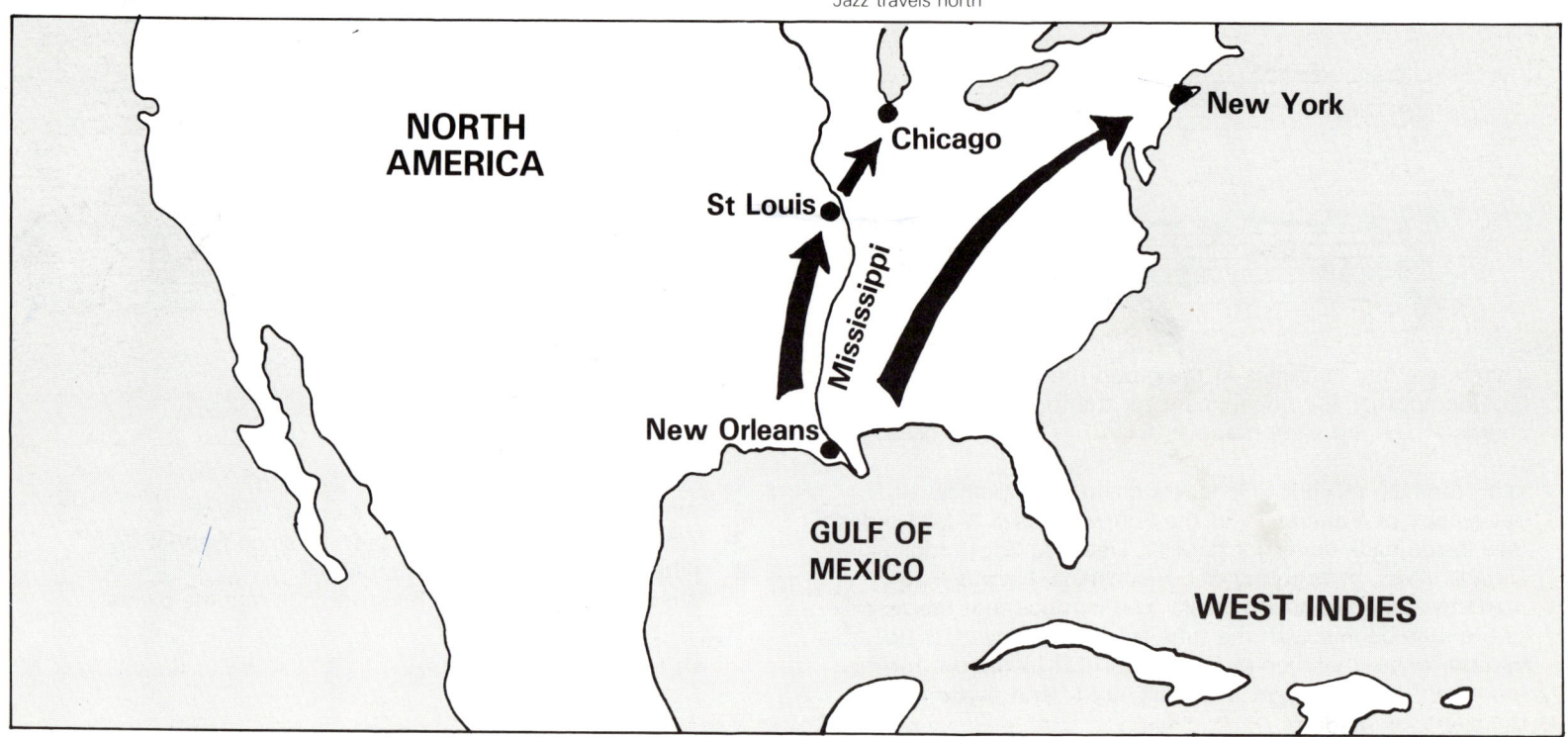

New Orleans remained the centre of jazz until 1918, when many of the bars and dance-halls in New Orleans were closed by order of the American navy. Jazz musicians lost their jobs, and left the city to find work elsewhere. They travelled northwards to **St Louis, Kansas, Chicago** and **New York**, taking the new music with them.

'We couldn't play soft'

Many jazzmen soon discovered that life was better in the north. As the bass player Arnold Loyacano said: 'They paid us 25 dollars a week in Chicago. The salary was the big thing. We'd been making a dollar a night down south in New Orleans'. But the music the jazz bands played remained as lively and loud as ever. Here's Arnold Loyacano's description of his first concert in Chicago:

> We couldn't play soft . . . . Didn't know what soft was. Here we come in with a trombone, clarinet and cornet . . . . People held their ears and yelled *too loud*. Well why not?

Jazz travels north

The New Orleans Rhythm Kings

The New Orleans Rhythm Kings

Soon Arnold Loyacano had joined one of the most famous of all jazz bands, the **New Orleans Rhythm Kings**. This band became so popular that people 'used to throw 100 dollar bills to keep them playing', and that often meant from eight at night until six o'clock the following morning.

Another well-known band was the **Original Dixieland Jazz Band**. Their *Dixie Jazz Band One-Step,* one of the first jazz recordings, was made in 1917. The band had begun by playing arrangements of piano ragtime pieces (see page 14) like Joplin's *Maple Leaf Rag,* and they became very popular in 1919 with their recording of *Tiger Rag.* But no-one could compete with the swinging sound of Louis Armstrong's band. Here's a description of it playing in St Louis in 1920:

> We cut loose with one of the very newest hot songs that had just been getting around home when we left — and we let it swing, plenty . . . . We almost split that room open — man, did we play!

Meade Lux Lewis

Boogie-woogie

Early in the 1920s a new kind of piano music became popular. It was called **boogie-woogie,** and used the same three basic chords as the Blues (see page 9). The pianist played fast repeated rhythms with his left hand. With his right he decorated the Blues chords. Complicated and exciting cross-rhythms between the hands resulted.

Boogie-woogie was played in clubs and at parties throughout Chicago in particular, during the 1920s. You could dance, as well as listen, to boogie music, as **Clarence Pine Top Smith** tells us on his recording of *Pine Top's Boogie-Woogie*:

> I want everybody to dance just like I tell ya.
> An' when I say 'Hold yourself'
> I want all of yer git ready to stop.
> An' when I say 'Stop' — Don't move.
> An' when I say 'Git it'
> I want all of you to do a boogie-woogie.

Other famous boogie-woogie pianists were **Charlie 'Cow Cow' Davenport** and **Meade Lux Lewis,** whose *Honky Tonk Train Blues* is one of the most popular boogie recordings ever.

'I'm so hungry . . . . I can't hardly speak'

At the end of the 1920s America was hit by an economic slump. Many people were thrown out of work, as factories ground to a halt. Jazz musicians had nowhere to play, as clubs and dance-halls closed. On the outskirts of Chicago and New York the penniless built shanty-towns out of packing cases and scraps of cardboard and metal. And they sang the Blues:

> I stood on the corner and almost bust ma head.
> I couldn't earn enough to buy me a loaf of bread.
> My gal's a house-maid, an' she earns a dollar a week.
> I'm so hungry on pay-day, I can't hardly speak.

Jobless workers on the march

Questions

1. Why did jazz musicians leave New Orleans in 1918?
2. The initials NORK stand for which famous jazz band?
3. Which band became famous with a recording of *Tiger Rag*?
4. What is the name of the new kind of piano music which became popular early in the 1920s?
5. Who recorded *Honky Tonk Train Blues*?

The kind of train that inspired Honky Tonk Train Blues

Projects

1. Here is an example of the kind of thing a boogie-woogie pianist plays with his left hand.
   Try playing the boogie bass yourself on melodica, tuned percussion, pitched low on the piano keyboard, or on any other instrument available. Then get your friends to join in. They should play the Blues chord sequence as shown on page 10.

2. With the help of your teacher (or using your local library), get a copy of the record *Boogie-woogie* (see inside back cover for details). Listen to *Honky Tonk Train Blues,* and notice how the pianist uses rhythms in his left hand similar to those you played in Project 1. Also, discuss with the rest of your group the ways in which the pianist imitates the sounds of a train.

Dancing to jazz in Chicago at the end of the 1920's ▶

3 Swing, be-bop and modern jazz

Swing arrangements

Before the days of swing, jazz bands usually contained about five players. Now they contained 12 or 13 musicians. Because of the large number of players involved, it was necessary for swing music to be **arranged** and written down. Years before, when the pianist Lil Hardin applied for a job with the New Orleans Creole Jazz Band, she was told that the band didn't need music. 'When you hear two knocks', the leader said, 'Just start playing'. It was just the opposite in swing: the details of the music had to be worked out and written down in advance. The players either had to be able to read music or be willing to learn their parts by ear.

Arranging popular songs and jazz favourites for the new swing bands was a skilful job. There were usually five instruments in the **brass** section, and four in each of the **saxophone** (see page 34) and **rhythm** sections. The arranger's job was to write parts for all of these instruments.

Lil Hardin with the Creole Jazz Band

Jitterbugs and bobbysoxers

It was some years before jazz musicians were able to find jobs once more. But by 1933 the economy had improved enough for clubs and dance-halls to re-open. And, as they re-opened, a new kind of jazz came into being, called **swing**. This new music used some old ingredients. It contained the 'call and response' pattern of worksongs (see page 8) and used blue notes (see page 9). You could hear the repeated rhythms of boogie-woogie (see page 18) in swing music, too. But the new music still sounded quite different from earlier jazz — and the reason was that it was played by much larger bands.

Benny Goodman

One of the best known swing arrangers was **Don Redman.** His arrangements were used by **Fletcher Henderson,** leader of the first of the big bands. In turn, Henderson's band influenced **Benny Goodman,** who became the 'King of Swing' in 1935:

> I called out some of our big Fletcher arrangements . . . and the boys seemed to get the idea. From the moment I kicked them off, they dug in with some of the best playing I'd heard . . . . The first big roar from the crowd was one of the sweetest sounds I ever heard in my life . . . .

Benny Goodman and his band

Typical of Goodman's band was its use of little, repeated snippets of tune called **riffs.** These riffs were passed from one section of the band to another in 'call and response' fashion (see page 8). After a while, this musical chit-chat became rather boring. So a solo player would add his own, more lively tune to the general musical conversation. But even when this happened, Goodman never let his soloists get out of hand. His band was carefully organized:

> I am . . . a bug on accuracy in performance, about playing in tune, and with just the proper note values in the written parts . . . .

Other famous band-leaders of the swing era were **Paul Whiteman** (see page 45) and **Count Basie.** Their music became popular in dance-halls throughout America. And the fans who danced to swing and bought records made by the swing bands became known as **jitterbugs** (because they jittered and jigged as they danced) and **bobbysoxers** (after the short white socks worn by the girls).

Paul Whiteman

Questions

1. What new kind of jazz came into being during the early 1930s?
2. How many players did the new jazz bands contain?
3. Name the three sections of a swing band.
4. Which earlier big band influenced Benny Goodman?
5. Name two swing band-leaders other than Benny Goodman.

Count Basie

Project

Here is a riff theme, typical of those used in swing. Play it through on melodicas, tuned percussion, piano or any other instruments. As you play notice how everything in the theme is based on the rhythm and melody of the first two bars:

Next divide into groups. Group 1 should play the riff theme while groups 2 and 3 play the Blues chord-sequence shown on page 10. (If you want to give your piece a boogie flavour, too, then a fourth group should add the boogie bass shown on page 19.)

Be-bop

Dizzy Gillespie

By the early 1940s a number of jazz musicians had grown tired of swing. They were bored with its riffs (see page 22) and felt limited by its carefully worked-out arrangements. They also felt that jazz was in danger of becoming nothing more than dance-music for bobbysoxers. So they invented a new form of jazz called **be-bop**, or **bop** for short.

Be-bop bands were much smaller than swing bands. Their smallness enabled individual instruments to be heard more easily. **Dizzy Gillespie** and **Charlie Parker** (nicknamed Bird) were leading be-bop musicians. They used much more complicated rhythms in their playing than swing musicians. These rhythms were often based on **Cuban music** (rumbas, congas, and cha-cha-chas), a new idea in jazz. In earlier jazz the drummer's job had been to make the beat clear. He used the low bass-drum and the side-drum (see page 37) for this purpose. But in be-bop the drummer played delicate rhythms on the **cymbal** (see page 37), using the drums as little as possible. As the pianist Lennie Tristano remarked at the time:

> Swing was hot, heavy and loud. Be-bop is cool, light and soft. Swing bumped and chugged along like a beat (worn-out) locomotive . . . . Be-bop has a more subtle beat . . . .
> Instead of a rhythm section pounding out each chord, four beats to a bar . . . the be-bop rhythm section uses a system of chordal punctuation.
> By this means, the soloist is able to hear the chord without having it shoved down his throat.
> He can think as he plays . . . .

The bass part in be-bop was played on a **string bass** (see page 36). It consisted of a fast-moving, never-ending series of notes, played **pizzicato** (see page 36).

The differences between swing and be-bop

SWING	BE-BOP
Large band	Small band
Arranged	Not arranged
Suitable for dancing	Not suitable for dancing
Riffs used	Riffs avoided
Firm drum beat	Delicate cymbal rhythms
Straightforward chords	Complicated chords
Played mostly on the beat	Played mostly off the beat
Bass line played at a moderate speed	Bass line played fast

'Dig them new sounds, man'

Be-bop bands used such well known pop songs as *I've got rhythm* as the basis of their music. But they left out the tune and made the chords more complicated. Often this resulted in 'wrong'-sounding notes being added to the chord. Here's trumpeter Miles Davis (see page 4):

> Every time I heard the chord of G . . . my fingers automatically took the position for C sharp on the instrument . . . .

In the end it became difficult, if not impossible, to recognize the original song.

Some older jazz musicians objected to this. One of them was Louis Armstrong (see page 4). He said:

> All the be-boppers want to do is show you up, and any old way will do as long as it's different from the way they played it before. So you get all them weird chords which don't mean nothing, and you got no melody to remember and no beat to dance to.

Of course, the be-boppers took no notice of these criticisms. Their attitude was summed up in the comment 'If you don't dig them new sounds, man you're real square!'

Playing it cool

On stage, the be-boppers took little notice of their audience. They walked on for a solo and dashed off showers of notes, as if it were the easiest thing in the world. Then they walked off again, ignoring any applause. Some musicians actually stood with their backs to the listeners as they played. Often they stopped playing in the middle of a phrase or chord-sequence, leaving it to the next soloist to pick up the pieces:

> . . . These cats snatched up their instruments and blew crazy stuff. One would stop all of a sudden and another would start for no reason at all. We never could tell when a solo was supposed to begin or end. Then they all quit and walked off the stand. It scared us . . .

Good playing in early jazz and swing had always been described as hot. Now it became the thing after a good be-bop solo to say 'Man, that was cool'. This expression became used of later jazz, too.

Charlie Parker

Questions

1. Which new form of jazz was invented early in the 1940s?
2. What were the differences between the new jazz and the old?
3. Which instrument played the bass part in the new jazz?
4. Why was it sometimes hard to recognize the songs upon which be-boopers based their music?
5. How was a good be-bop solo described?

Projects

1. When Miles Davis heard a G chord he played a C sharp against it, at least in the days of be-bop. Here's an experiment to show what a discordant effect Miles produced. Get some friends to play a G chord. This consists of the notes G, b and d:

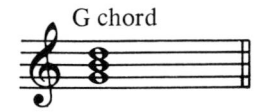

   G chord

   Get your friends to repeat the chord to a firm beat. And, as they play, add a C sharp of your own now and again:

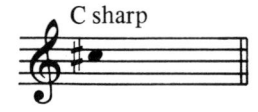

   C sharp

   Then ask your friends to play the complete Blues chord sequence. And you can try adding an F sharp to the C chord:

   C chord   F sharp

Miles Davis

   Not to mention a B to the F chord:

   F chord   B

2. With the help of your teacher (or using your local library), get a copy of Volume 11 of the Folkways Jazz record series (see inside back cover for details). Play the recording by the Dizzy Gillespie Sextet of *Groovin' High* and listen out for the fast-moving string bass part so typical of be-bop. The band begins by playing the *Groovin' High* theme. Notice how the piano keeps echoing the last two notes of the saxophone phrases. There then follow some solos based on the theme. The most important of these are the solos by Charlie Parker on alto saxophone (see page 34) and Dizzy Gillespie on trumpet (see page 35). Which of these solos do you prefer and why? Between the solos there is a short section during which the string bass is played with a bow rather than pizzicato (see page 36). Notice how different it sounds. The final solo on the recording is played on an electric instrument (see page 37). What is it called?

Modern jazz

Modern Jazz Quartet

In 1949 Miles Davis (see page 4) released an album called *Birth of the Cool*. Although based on be-bop style, the music on the new album was easier to listen to than Miles' earlier music. It was the beginning of what became called **modern jazz**.

Other players, like the saxophonist Gerry Mulligan, and arrangers like Gil Evans, also moved from be-bop to modern jazz. The new style used simpler rhythms and harmonies than bop. It had an easy-going beat. And musicians played '. . . in lag-along style, where you relax . . . .' The music was more tuneful and players used fewer bop-style 'wrong notes' (see page 25). They also used less of the **vibrato** which was typical of be-bop. (*Vibrato* means the quick, repeated change of a pitch of a note.) Early in the 1950s the West Coast of America became a centre for the new jazz.

Third stream

Saxophonist **Paul Desmond** joined with pianist **Dave Brubeck** in adding to their jazz ideas from classical music (see pages 44-48). West Coast musicians began using classical instruments, too: for example, **French horn, flute** and **cello**. Soon other jazz musicians followed their lead. In New York the **Modern Jazz Quartet** included arrangements of classical pieces in their concerts. Lead by pianist John Lewis, the Modern Jazz Quartet (or 'MJQ' as it was nicknamed) included double bass, drums and vibraphone (see page 37). Other musicians soon began bringing classical music and jazz together. This new style was called **Third Stream** music.

French horn

Flute

Cello

The new wave

Miles Davis continued to be an important influence on modern jazz during the 1960s. His album *Miles in the sky* broke with tradition because he used electric piano (see page 37), and replaced double bass with **electric bass guitar**. Jazz musicians had always been rather snobbish about these instruments, which they believed were only suitable for pop music. But Davis invited **Chick Corea** to play electric piano for him, and since then Chick has become one of today's most important figures in jazz. His albums (including *Return to forever*) are very popular.

Another important musician in modern jazz is **Thelonius Monk**. One of the original be-boppers, Monk's style of piano-playing became famous during the 1960s. He played sparingly: he never used more notes than were necessary, and filled his music with jerky, off-beat rhythms. **Sonny Rollins** admired Monk's playing and imitated his style on the saxophone.

Thelonius Monk

John Coltrane

Experimental sounds

In the search for new sounds some modern jazz musicians experimented with new ways of playing their instruments. **Ornette Coleman** began using a plastic saxophone because he liked its shrill tone. **Roland Kirk** produced new effects by singing and making other sounds as he played the flute. Kirk also became famous for playing two or even three wind instruments at once, while **John Coltrane** managed to play two or three notes at once on one instrument, the tenor saxophone. ('It's done', he explained, 'by false fingering and adjusting your lips . . .') Coltrane's playing pushed 'his instrument beyond any previous limits of sound possibilities'. In the process he produced 'high-pitched squeals, braying yawps' and 'screams' from his instrument.

Jazz today

Jazz today is made up of several different styles. The first reason for this is simple: some of the musicians who helped shape the history of jazz still perform today, and so their styles live on. The second reason is that many musicians of today have begun copying the sounds of the old New Orleans bands ('traditional' or 'trad' jazz), or the bands of the swing era. The third reason is that several musicians have taken ideas from recent jazz and combined these with still newer ideas. These are the musicians who could really be said to play 'the jazz of our time'. The different styles to be found in jazz today are reflected in the different kinds of band which exist. Here is some information about these bands and their styles.

Acker Bilk

▲ Kenny Ball with his band

The traditional jazz band

These bands are the result of our modern interest in early jazz, the music of New Orleans and the 1920s. There are usually at least seven musicians in such bands, playing clarinet, trumpet, trombone, banjo, piano, string bass and percussion (see pages 34-37). The main tune is given to the trumpet, while the clarinet and trombone each play contrasting melodies. The rest of the band lays down a firm beat in imitation of the sound of the old marching bands (see pages 12-13). You can hear many modern 'revival' bands of this kind in New Orleans today. British examples include the bands led by **Kenny Ball** and **Acker Bilk**.

Swing bands

These bands imitate the sound of the swing bands of the 1930s. They are just as large, and sometimes even larger, with five trumpets, five trombones and five saxophones, piano, electric bass guitar and percussion. Modern swing bands make the most of the riffs (see page 22) and the 'call and response' patterns (see page 8) of the original bands.

Two popular modern swing bands are led by **Woody Hermann** and **Buddy Rich.** Many colleges and schools in America have swing bands, too, often of a high standard. In England the best known band of this type is the **National Youth Jazz Orchestra. Duke Ellington's** music is based on swing, but also uses ideas from later jazz. In Britain Mike Gibbs has been influenced by Ellington. He uses the instruments in his band sparingly, keeping the big-band effect for the most important moments.

Small bands

One of the most famous small bands of today is the Modern Jazz Quartet (see page 27). The MJQ has now been playing for over 25 years, and its music is admired by many jazz musicians. One of these is England's **Graham Collier,** who

Duke Ellington and his band

Chicago in concert

wrote 'The level of musical interest they achieve, by means of clever writing and superb musicianship, is astounding'.

Collier's own compositions are a mixture of Third Stream (see page 27) and New Wave jazz (see page 28). He also takes ideas from other kinds of music. The most important of these is the way he uses scales from **folk music.** Many of his pieces use riffs (see page 22), chords and melodies based on these scales, which are called **modes.**

Free-form jazz

Some present-day musicians have taken up **free-form** jazz. In this kind of music (played by the **Spontaneous Music Ensemble**, for example) 'anything goes'. There is often no obvious chord or melodic pattern. The players make their music up on the spot (**extemporize**) without controls. Often they choose a mood or idea, and express it in their extemporizations.

Jazz-pop bands

These bands play arrangements of pop songs. The arrangements are often complicated and make use of jazz-style harmonies and instruments. Such bands include the American **Blood, Sweat and Tears,** and **Chicago**.

Other musicians wishing to link jazz with pop (see pages 41-43) take ideas from pop as the basis of their extemporizations. They use the simpler riffs and chord sequences of pop, and feature pop-style electric instruments in their bands. Examples include the British **Soft Machine** and **Nucleus**.

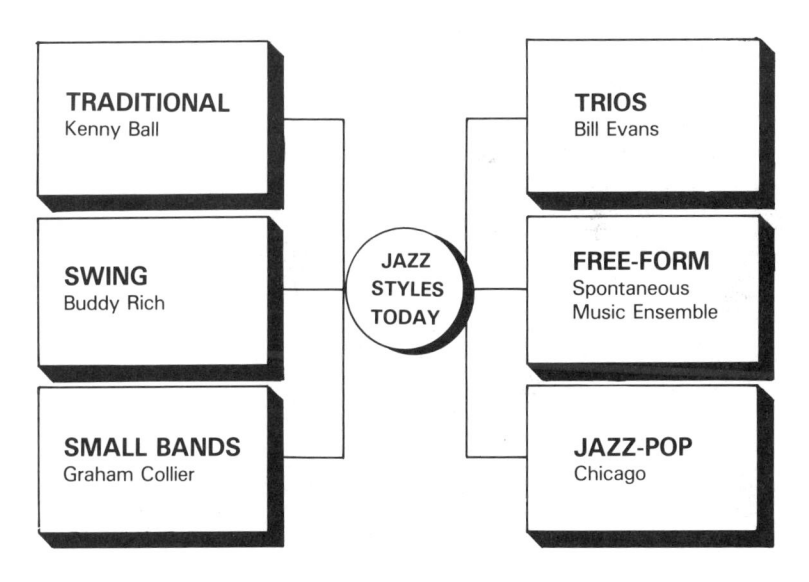

Trios

Jazz bands with no more than three members are common today. These bands are called **trios**. Usually the leader plays piano, and is accompanied by string bass and percussion. Most of the work in such trios falls on the pianist. The bass and percussion players support the pianist with rhythm and drive; they also join in with their own musical ideas. Famous piano trios are led by the Englishman **George Shearing,** the American **Bill Evans** and the Canadian **Oscar Petersen**.

```
TRADITIONAL                        TRIOS
Kenny Ball                         Bill Evans

SWING              JAZZ            FREE-FORM
Buddy Rich         STYLES          Spontaneous
                   TODAY           Music Ensemble

SMALL BANDS                        JAZZ-POP
Graham Collier                     Chicago
```

Questions

1. Which album started modern jazz?
2. What is Third Stream music?
3. Who made an album called *Return to forever*?
4. Who produced 'squeals, yawps and screams' from his saxophone?
5. Name the leader of a British traditional jazz band of today.
6. Which country does the National Youth Jazz Orchestra belong to?
7. What is a mode?
8. What is a piano trio?
9. What kind of jazz does the Spontaneous Music Ensemble play?
10. Name two jazz-pop bands.

Projects

1. With the help of your teacher, or through your local library, get a copy of the Modern Jazz Quartet album *Blues on Bach* (see inside back cover for details). Listen to 'Don't stop this train' (side 2, band 3), which is an arrangement of a piece by J S Bach. Then think about these questions:
   (a) Which keyboard instrument used on the recording was common in the time of Bach?
   (b) What's the name of the electric instrument used?
   (c) Which instrument plays the bass part?
   Ask your teacher to play you a classical recording of the same piece, and see what the differences are between the classical and jazz performances. Which do you prefer?
2. Graham Collier makes use of folk modes in his compositions. Here is the D mode written out for you:

   D e f g a b c D

   Make up a tune of your own using the mode. Your tune should be in four-time. And remember to stop and start the tune on the note which gives the mode its name.
3. Here is a bass riff similar to those used by jazz-pop bands. Play it through on whatever instruments you have, the lower-pitched the better:

   Then get some friends to add these accompaniments:

count	① 2 3 4	② 2 3 4
instruments 1	a f	f D
instruments 2	D D	D

   Finally get someone else to play the riff and add the D mode tune you made up in Project 2.

Blood, Sweat & Tears

4 Jazz instruments

Musical instruments used in jazz come from each of the four families: **woodwind, brass, strings** and **percussion**.

Clarinet

Woodwind

The **clarinet** is often used in swing and traditional jazz bands. The sound is made when the player blows on to a reed fitted into the mouthpiece of the instrument. Another reed instrument, the **saxophone,** is used in swing and modern jazz bands. It comes in four different sizes. These are named after the human voices: soprano, alto, tenor and bass. The soprano saxophone is the smallest and highest in pitch, the bass the biggest and lowest in pitch. The alto and tenor saxophones are the most frequently used.

Flutes are sometimes used in modern jazz bands. These instruments do not have reeds. Instead the player blows across a small hole near one end of the instrument.

Ornette Coleman playing the saxophone

Brass

The most common brass instrument in jazz today is the high-pitched **trumpet**. The **fluegelhorn** and **cornet** are also popular. They have a similar range to the trumpet. The cornet was very popular in early jazz bands.

On all these instruments, the player changes notes by pressing down valves on the top of the instrument. But on the lower-pitched **trombone**, changes are made by moving a long slide in and out of the instrument. For this reason a trombonist needs plenty of space around him as he plays.

The problem of space was solved in an amusing way by the early touring bands in New Orleans. These bands toured the streets in waggons, especially at Mardi Gras time (see page 12). And the trombonists always sat at the opposite end of the waggon to the horses. This was so that the slides of their instruments could extend beyond the end (or the tailgate) of the waggon. Also to be found in these old bands were low-pitched **tubas**. Today some traditional and swing bands make use of these large instruments.

The cornet was played by Bix Beiderbecke (see page 44)

mostly for rhythmic chord-playing.

In early jazz the **banjo** was used for the same purpose. This instrument produces a brighter tone than the guitar. Strings on the banjo are stretched across a metal frame. This is covered over with parchment on top and left open underneath.

The piano is a keyboard instrument. The strings are hit with felt-covered hammers controlled by the black and white keys. Like the guitar, the piano is often used for rhythmic chord-playing in jazz.

The **double bass** is the largest of all instruments. In jazz it is usually played pizzicato (i.e. the strings are plucked). But sometimes the strings are stroked with a horse-hair bow.

How many of the instruments in Bunk Johnson's band can you name?

Electric guitar

Strings

String instruments common in jazz include the **guitar, double bass** and **piano.** In each of them sounds are made when thin strands of wire or gut are caused to vibrate. To make the sound carry, the strings are stretched across a hollow **soundbox** (or, in the case of the piano, a **soundboard**). The guitar-player plucks the strings with the fingers of one hand. He produces different notes by pressing down the strings at different points against a fingerboard with the other. In jazz today, the guitar is used

Percussion

The drummer in a jazz band often uses over 12 different percussion instruments. His jobs are to set the style and speed of the music, and to keep the players in time with each other. To do this he uses a number of **drums** and **cymbals,** hitting these instruments with sticks, beaters or wire brushes. The drums include snare-drums (also called side-drums), large and small tom-toms and bass drum. The bass drum is operated by the drummer's foot (by means of a pedal-beater). The hi-hat is also operated by the drummer's foot. It consists of two cymbals on a stand. They are clashed together when the player pushes down a pedal connected to them by rods. A number of other, different sized, cymbals are also part of a drummer's kit. These are mounted on floor stands or on the bass drum. Other percussion instruments used by the drummer include **tambourine** and **maracas.**

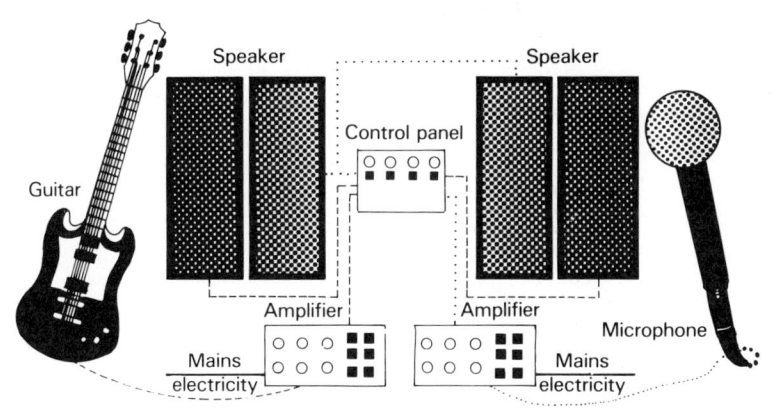

Many bands amplify their instruments

As you might expect, with all these instruments, a drummer can make a great deal of noise. Partly for this reason, many jazz bands today use **amplification.** In performance, microphones are either placed close to, or attached to, the saxophones, trumpets and other instruments mentioned above. Jazz singers (see page 38) also use microphones. Sounds picked up by the mikes are passed to an amplifier, which makes them louder, and then feeds them through loudspeakers. Some jazz bands use instruments which are made specially to be played through loudspeakers. These instruments have come into jazz from pop music. They include electric piano and guitar (see page 28).

Vibraphones are found in some bands. The vibraphone is like a large glockenspiel in appearance. Sounds are produced when the metal keys are hit with beaters. Tubes underneath the keys make the sound louder. They also contain discs which are made to revolve electrically. These create the vibrato effect (see page 27) which is typical of the instrument.

style with their voices. After singing the words and tune of a popular song, they could 'take off', extemporizing (see page 31) with their voices in the same way as instrumentalists. There are many records of scat-singing. Louis Armstrong's *Skid-dat-de-dat* is one of the most exciting.

Whether 'scatting' or not, jazz singers have always used their voices more adventurously than most pop singers. Listen, for example, to Billie Holiday. Her voice was once described as '. . . one of the incomparable sounds that jazz has produced . . . .' Her style of singing was a mixture of those of Louis Armstrong and the Blues singer Bessie Smith (see page 9). (Billie Holiday's singing-style in turn was imitated by several players of jazz instruments, for example saxophonist **Lester Young**.) Other famous jazz singers include **Ella Fitzgerald** and **Cleo Laine**.

Billie Holiday

Cleo Laine

Jazz singers

Some jazz musicians are famous both as singers and instrumentalists. For example, Louis Armstrong was as well known for his gravelly-sounding voice as for his brilliant trumpet-playing. In fact, his singing style was affected by the style of his playing. One day, the story goes, he forgot the words of a song as he was singing it. And on the spur of the moment he invented nonsense-syllables in place of the words. This kind of singing, called **scat-singing,** soon caught on with other jazz musicians. It was a way of imitating instrumental

Questions

1. Name the four families of instruments.
2. What is the smallest saxophone called?
3. Which is the most common brass instrument in jazz today?
4. Is the tuba a high- or low-pitched instrument?
5. Name three string instruments used in jazz.
6. What does pizzicato mean?
7. What is a hi-hat?
8. What is an amplifier for?
9. What is scat-singing?
10. Whose voice was described as 'incomparable'?

Projects

1. Collect information about some of the instruments mentioned on pages 34-37. Copy up the information and put it into a folder together with pictures of the instruments wherever possible.
2. Here are two examples of scat-singing rhythms. Try speaking them through firmly to a steady beat:

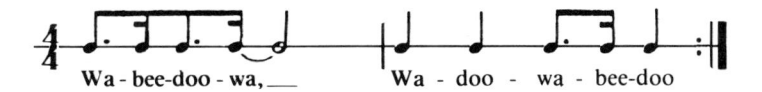

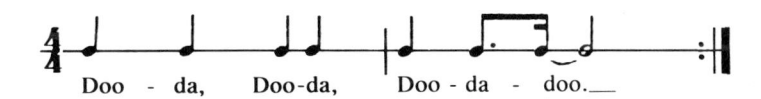

   Wa - bee-doo - wa,___ Wa - doo - wa - bee-doo

   Doo - da, Doo-da, Doo - da - doo.___

   You can also clap the rhythms or play them on untuned percussion instruments. Teach the rhythms to a friend. And then speak or play them both together. Finally, make up some scat rhythms of your own.

Louis Armstrong

3. Ella Fitzgerald's recording of *Jersey Bounce* (on *Jazz Spectrum Volume 12* — see back cover for details) contains some exciting scat-singing. Borrow a copy of the record from your local library and write down your version of the nonsense-syllables Ella sings.

   The same album also has some songs performed by Billie Holiday on it. Listen to her version of *Cheek to cheek,* a song which was composed by Irving Berlin (see page 42), and compare Billie Holiday's voice with Ella Fitzgerald's. Which voice do you prefer and why? Write out a list of the instruments which accompany Billie Holiday.
4. With the help of your teacher, or through your local library, obtain a copy of a recent Cleo Laine album. Listen to the album and then write a sleeve note for it. This should be short and designed to make the reader want to buy the record. You might mention, for example, the things that appeal to you about Cleo Laine's singing; or draw attention to a song that you enjoy particularly; or mention instrumental effects that you think work well.

5 Jazz and other kinds of music

Jazz and popular music

Cole Porter

Jazz has always been an important influence on popular music. Since jazz began dance-bands have been modelled on jazz bands, and popular songs have been modelled on the Blues (see page 9). Blue notes (see page 9), jazz rhythms and riffs (see page 22) can all be found in popular music, usually in a simpler form. Many popular entertainers began as jazz singers or players. Good examples are the band-leader **Glenn Miller** and the singer **Billie Holiday** (see page 38).

In return, popular music has provided much material for jazz musicians. As pianist Fats Waller said 'You gotta have melody', and the melodies of famous pop songs have long been the starting point for jazz extemporizations (see page 31). Jerome Kern's *Smoke gets in your eyes*, Jack Strachey's *These foolish things* and Cole Porter's *Night and day* are three examples of such songs. Another pop music influence on jazz is the use of electric instruments (see page 37).

Musicals

Many famous American pop songs come from musicals (short for musical comedies). These are plays or films in which the most important moments are brought alive by singing. The singers are accompanied by an orchestra. And the style of the music owes much to jazz. *Smoke gets in your eyes,* for example, is a song from Jerome Kern's musical *Showboat*, first performed in 1927.

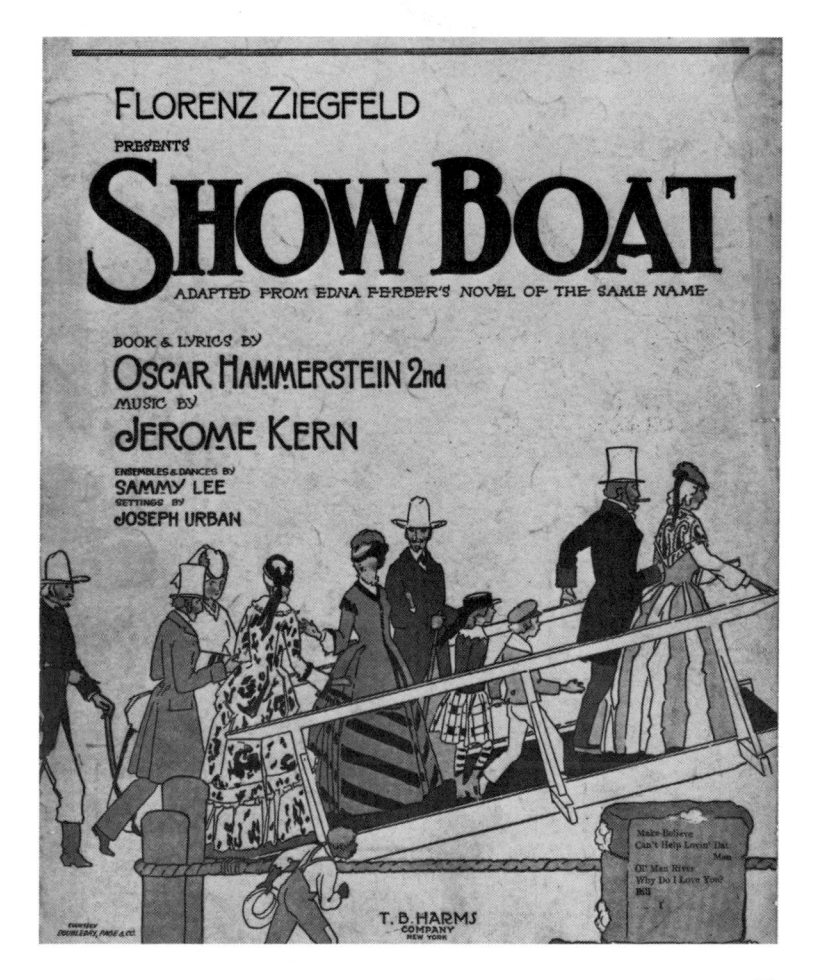

▲ Irving Berlin with some friends

Irving Berlin

Irving Berlin was one of the most famous of all American composers of musicals. His well known musicals include *Annie get your gun* and *Call me madam.* His first job as a musician was as a singing waiter in New York, early this century. As a result of this Berlin became skilled at making up tunes which people could remember easily. But since he had no training in harmony Berlin usually played the tunes with one finger on the piano to other musicians, and got them to add chords to his songs.

Because many of Irving Berlin's songs had the same basic shape (or **form** as it is called), there was a rumour that he had invented a song-making machine. This was supposed to be able to turn out song melodies by the dozen, all identical in form. Certainly Berlin's songs *were* usually 32 bars long and in **ternary form**.

Writing songs for fun

Cole Porter's musical *Anything goes* is full of jazz ideas. Jazz rhythms and harmonies, ideas taken from spirituals (see page 7) and boogie-woogie (see page 18) can all be found in this musical. Unlike Irving Berlin, Cole Porter had been trained in classical music, and so could harmonize his own tunes. He found composing easy. In fact, once he admitted that he '. . . wrote songs for fun . . .' And many people would say that listening to his compositions is fun, too. There are plenty of good tunes in his musical *Kiss me Kate.* (And you'll find an arrangement of one of them on page 43.)

The heyday of the musical was the period 1940-50. Frank Loesser's *Guys and dolls,* and Rodgers and Hammerstein's *Oklahoma!* were first performed then.

Questions

1. Who said 'You gotta have melody'?
2. Name a pop song often used as a starting point for jazz extemporizations.
3. When was Jerome Kern's *Showboat* first performed?
4. Which composer was supposed to have invented a song-making machine?
5. Which of these musicals was composed by Cole Porter: *Guys and dolls, Kiss me Kate, Oklahoma!*?

Project

Below you'll find part of a tune from *Kiss me Kate*. Play it through on any suitable instrument that's available. As you play listen for jazz influences, like the many blue notes (marked *):

Next practise the tune and the accompaniment (see below) with some friends. (The accompaniment is basically the same as the original one. Notice the boogie-woogie influence.) Finally, divide into two groups and play tune and accompaniment together.

Jazz and classical music

Igor Stravinsky

In 1922 the French classical composer **Darius Milhaud** visited a jazz club in New York. The club was in the Harlem district of the city. And Milhaud was bowled over by the music he heard:

> . . . Against the beat of the drums the melodic lines criss-crossed in a breathless pattern of broken and twisted rhythms . . . . The effect of this music was so overwhelming that I could not tear myself away . . .

At once Milhaud decided to bring elements of jazz into his music. He wrote some *Rag Caprices* for piano. In them he imitated ragtime rhythms (see page 14). He also composed a ballet (*The creation of the world*) mixing ideas from classical music and jazz. In the ballet he used blue notes (see page 9) and jazz harmonies. He also added jazz instruments (for example saxophone and hi-hat) to the classical orchestra.

The threepenny opera

Other European classical composers took ideas from jazz, too. **Stravinsky** imitated the sound of a jazz band in his 1918 stage-work *The soldier's tale*. Like Milhaud, Stravinsky was interested in ragtime and wrote some pieces based on this style. The German composer **Kurt Weill** used jazz instruments, melodies and harmonies in his famous *Threepenny opera*. (One of its tunes, *Mack the knife,* became an instant hit, and is still often heard.)

Bix Beiderbecke

Some jazz musicians have taken ideas from classical music. One of the most famous early jazz players, **Bix Beiderbecke**, admired the music of Debussy (a French composer who died in 1918). Beiderbecke imitated Debussy's style of tunes in his cornet-playing, and used Debussy-style chords in his piano playing. These chords have remained part of jazz to this day. Other classical ideas can be heard in the recordings of the Third Stream bands of the 1950s (see page 27).

George Gershwin

In 1924 an important concert took place in New York, at the Aeolian Hall. This was a classical concert hall. But bandleader Paul Whiteman had decided to put on a concert there to show '... the advance which had been made from discordant early jazz to the melodious form of the present ....' The climax of the concert was the first performance of a piece of music called *Rhapsody in blue.* This had been written by **George Gershwin**, the first American composer to link jazz and classical music. *Rhapsody in blue* is scored for piano and orchestra. And, as you'll have guessed from its title, Gershwin used blue notes (see page 9) to give a jazzy flavour to his melodies and harmonies. He also uses catchy jazz rhythms, and sometimes writes in ragtime style for the piano. Even so, Gershwin designed his piece to be played on classical instruments by classically-trained musicians. The form of *Rhapsody in blue* is also classical. So the piece is neither completely jazz nor completely classical in style. It's a mixture of the two.

Porgy and Bess

Gershwin's most famous work is his opera *Porgy and Bess.* This was first performed in 1935. In it he again shows great skill in combining ideas from jazz and classical music.

Today *Porgy and Bess* is recognized as one of the finest of all American operas. But the critics at its first performance in New York had mixed feelings about it. One described the hit songs, such as *Summertime,* as 'sure-fire rubbish'. Another said that Gershwin's music was '... of our own soil and of our own days', and went on to say that *Porgy and Bess* was 'a joy for Americans to hear'.

Scenes from Porgy & Bess

Down on Catfish Row

Porgy and Bess is set in the South Carolina seaport of Charleston. The main characters live in the run-down **Catfish Row** area of the city, and are all black. And, for this reason, the music is based on the music of black Americans, the jazz of the 1920s and 1930s. In it you can hear Blues chord patterns (see page 9), riffs (see page 22) and boogie-woogie (see page 18). Gershwin also brings in the sound of spirituals (see page 7). And he imitates the cries of the Catfish Row street sellers: 'I'm talkin' about food I sell', sings the crab man, 'talkin' about devil crab, she crab'.

Picnic on Kittiwah Island

One of the most exciting scenes in the opera takes place on **Kittiwah Island.** Some of the people from Catfish Row have gone to the island for a picnic. Everyone's determined to have a good time, making music, dancing, 'doin' what they like to do'. To set the scene Gershwin uses African drums (see page 6). These play lively cross rhythms taken from negro folk music. Members of the cast join in, playing mouth organs, combs, jawbones (see page 6), a washboard and a washtub. Then **Sporting Life,** one of the opera's main characters, leads the chorus in some frenzied 'call and response' singing (see page 8). 'Wadoo', he calls out savagely, using the nonsense syllables of scat-singing (see page 38). 'Wadoo', responds the chorus. 'Zim bam boddle-oo, Hoodle ah da wa wa, Scatty wa', he goes on, with the rest of the singers imitating the rhythms and blue notes he uses.

All too soon we hear the whistle of the steamboat come to take everyone home. 'Hurry up', Bess is told, 'dat boat's gettin' de whoopin' cough'. And before long Kittiwah Island becomes quiet once more. (Or nearly — for some of the visitors miss the boat. But that's another story . . .)

West Side Story

Many other American classical composers have used jazz ideas. **Aaron Copland** and **Leonard Bernstein** are two of the best known. Listen, for example, to Copland's Piano Concerto, which borrows directly from jazz, or to his Clarinet Concerto, written for Benny Goodman, the 'King of Swing' himself (see page 22). There are jazz ideas in Bernstein's popular musical *West Side Story*. These include the use of blue notes and Blues form (see page 9), offbeat jazz rhythms and riffs (see page 22).

West Side Story was first performed in 1957 when it was described as a 'sensational hit' and a 'super-modern musical drama'. The drama is set in the slums of New York. Here two rival teenage gangs, the Jets and the Sharks, are 'at war' with each other. When one of the Jets, Tony, falls in love with Maria from the Sharks you might think their affair would end the war. But no. In the frenzy of a fight between the gangs Tony is forced into murdering Maria's brother. And then Tony is himself shot in a counter-attack.

Many of the songs from *West Side Story* have been big hits. Have you heard *Maria* or *Tonight*?

Project

Here's a tune from *Porgy and Bess,* 'I got plenty o' nuttin'':

Play it on recorders, melodicas, tuned percussion or any other instruments. (If there are some guitarists in your group, get them to play the chords shown above the tune as an accompaniment.) If you have musicians to spare divide them into two groups so that they can add the accompaniments shown below. One group should play the Instruments 1 part on higher-pitched instruments. The other should use the lowest-pitched instruments available to play the Instruments 2 part:

Questions

1. Why did Milhaud decide to bring elements of jazz into his music?
2. Who wrote *The soldier's tale*?
3. Which composer influenced Bix Beiderbecke?
4. List the instruments played by the visitors to Kittiwah Island.
5. Which piece of music was described as a 'sensational hit'?